Alligators • Caimanes

ALICE TWINE

TRADUCCIÓN AL ESPAÑOL:
José María Obregón

PowerKiDS press & **Editorial Buenas Letras**™
New York

Published in 2008 by The Rosen Publishing Group, Inc.
29 East 21st Street, New York, NY 10010

First Edition

Editor: Amelie von Zumbusch
Book Design: Julio Gil
Photo Researcher: Nicole Pristash

Photo Credits: Cover, pp. 1, 5, 7, 9, 11, 13, 17, 19, 21, 23, 24 (top left, top right, bottom left, bottom right) Shutterstock.com; p. 15 © Chris Johns/Getty Images.

Cataloging Data

Twine, Alice.
  Alligators–Caimanes / Alice Twine; traducción al español: José María Obregón. — 1st ed.
     p. cm. — (Baby animals–Animales bebé)
  ISBN-13: 978-1-4042-7682-6 (library binding)
  ISBN-10: 1-4042-7682-3 (library binding)
  1. Alligators–Infancy—Juvenile literature. 2. Spanish language materials I. Title.

Manufactured in the United States of America.

Websites: Due to the changing nature of Internet links, PowerKids Press and Editorial Buenas Letras have developed an online list of Web sites related to the subject of this book. This site is updated regularly. Please use this link to access the list: www.powerkidslinks.com/baby/all/

Contents

Contenido

Can you guess what this small animal is? It is a baby alligator!

¿Sabes que animal es éste? ¡Es un bebé caimán!

4

Newborn alligators are only 6 to 8 inches (15–20 cm) long. However, adult alligators are often as long as 13 feet (4 m)!

Los caimanes recién nacidos miden entre 6 y 8 pulgadas (15–20 cm) de largo. ¡Al crecer, los caimanes pueden tener hasta 13 pies (4 m) de largo!

Baby alligators have yellow **stripes** on their skin. They will lose these stripes as they grow up.

Los bebés caimán tienen **rayas** amarillas en la piel. Al crecer, las rayas desaparecen.

Alligators have a rounded **snout**. They have lots of sharp teeth. Alligators use their teeth to catch food.

Los caimanes tienen un **hocico** redondeado. Los caimanes también tienen dientes filosos. Los caimanes usan los dientes para comer.

10

Alligators live in watery places, such as rivers, lakes, and **wetlands**.

Los caimanes viven en lugares con mucha humedad, como ríos, lagos y **pantanos**.

Mother alligators lay many eggs. After about two months, baby alligators break out of the eggs.

Las mamás caimán ponen muchos huevos. Después de dos meses, los bebés caimán salen de los huevos.

14

Alligator mothers watch over their babies. The mothers keep the babies safe from animals that might want to eat them.

Las mamás caimán cuidan a sus bebés. Las mamás los cuidan para que otros animales no se los coman.

16

Alligators swim quietly through the water to catch their food. Young alligators eat bugs, small fish, frogs, and mice.

Los caimanes nadan en silencio para atrapar su comida. Los caimanes más jóvenes comen insectos, peces pequeños, ranas y ratones.

18

As all alligators do, baby alligators like to lie around in the sun.

Como a todos los caimanes, a los caimanes bebé les gusta tumbarse al sol.

20

Adult alligators live alone, but young alligators stick together. They form groups, called **pods**.

Los caimanes adultos viven solos, pero los caimanes jóvenes viven en grupos. Estos grupos se llaman **manadas**.

Words to Know • Palabras que debes saber

pod / (la) manada

snout / (el) hocico

stripes / (las) rayas

wetlands / (los) pantanos